ANIMALIA

Graeme Base

Within the pages of this book
You may discover, if you look
Beyond the spell of written words,
A hidden land of beasts and birds.

For many things are 'of a kind',
And those with keenest eyes will find
A thousand things, or maybe more—
It's up to you to keep the score.

A final word before we go;
There's one more thing you ought to know:
In Animalia, you see,
It's possible you might find *me*.

— Graeme

For Robyn

Harry N. Abrams, Inc., Publishers, New York

ISBN 0-8109-1868-4   Copyright © Graeme Base, 1986   A Robert Sessions Book

An Armoured Armadillo Avoiding An Angry Alligator

GREAT GREEN GORILLAS GROWING GRAPES IN A GORGEOUS GLASS GREENHOUSE

Horrible hairy hogs

hurrying homeward on heavily-harnessed horses

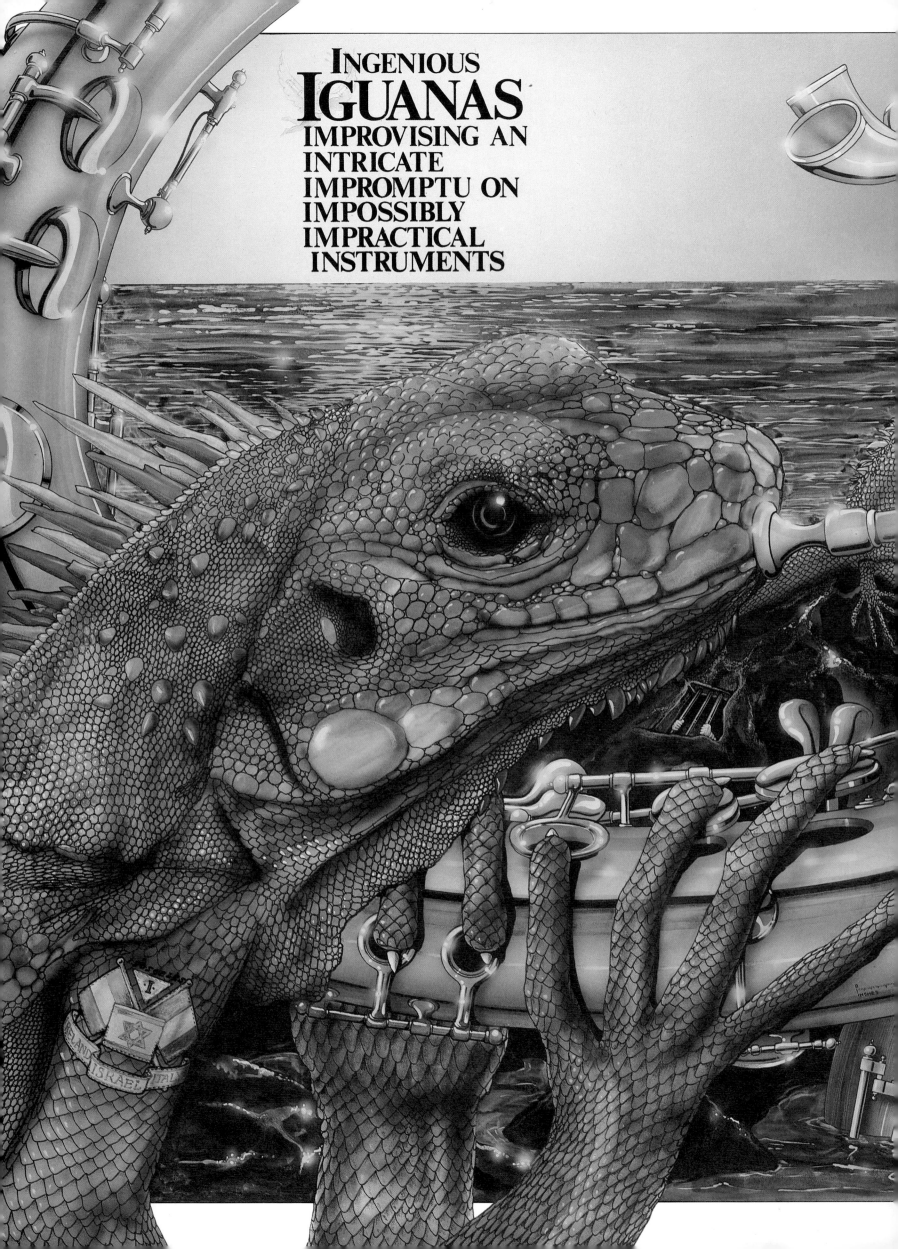

Ingenious IGUANAS

IMPROVISING AN INTRICATE IMPROMPTU ON IMPOSSIBLY IMPRACTICAL INSTRUMENTS

· JOVIAL · JACKALS · JUGGLING · JUGS · OF · JELLY · IN · THE · JUNGLE ·

?123+=METICULOUS MICE MONITORING MYSTERIOUS MATHEMATICAL MESSAGES

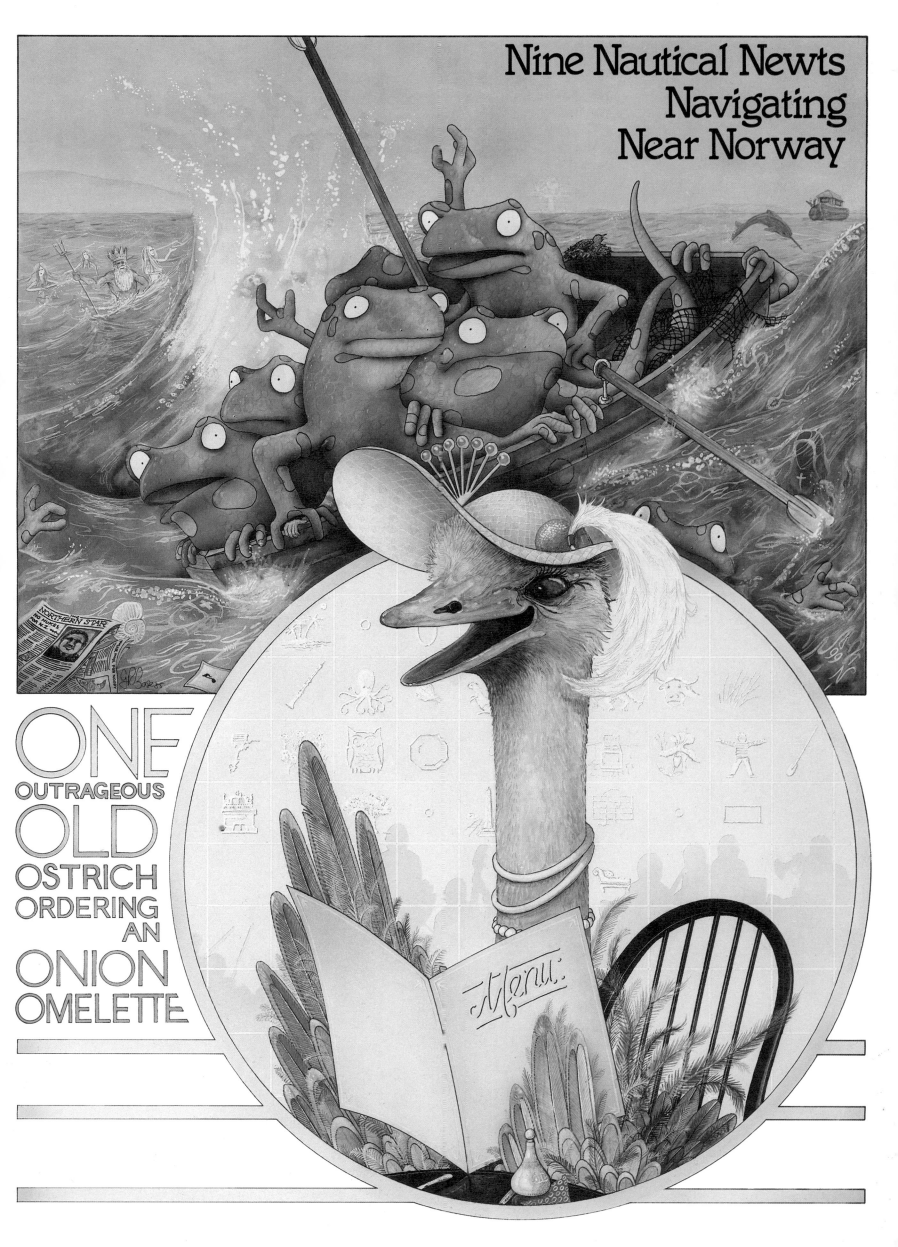

Nine Nautical Newts
Navigating
Near Norway

ONE
OUTRAGEOUS
OLD
OSTRICH
ORDERING
AN
ONION
OMELETTE

Quivering Quails Queuing Quietly for Quills

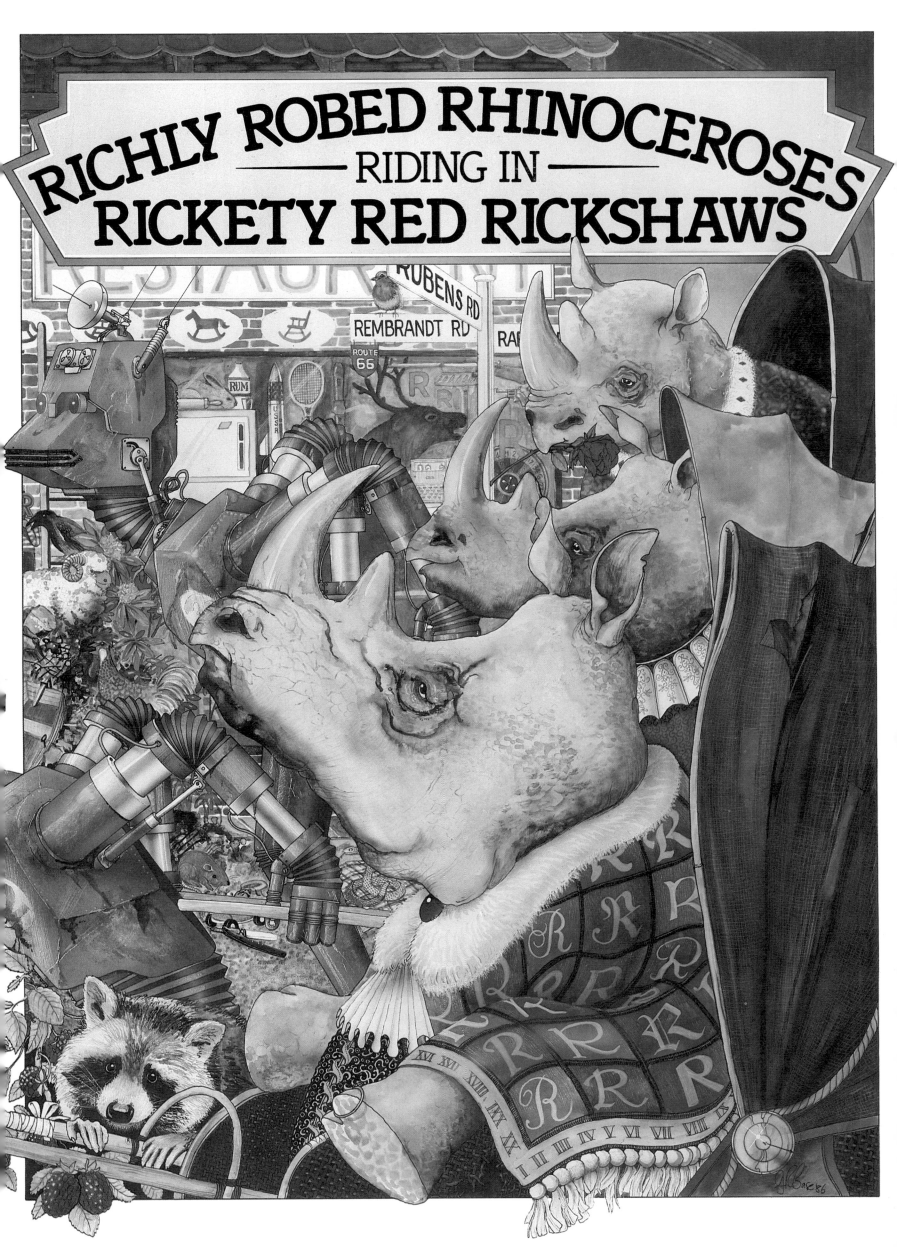

SIX · SLITHERING · SNAKES

SLIDING · SILENTLY · SOUTHWARD

THE LIBRARY

Nazareth

College Of Rochester

"A precious--mouldering pleasure --'tis
To meet an Antique Book--
In just the Dress his Century wore--
privilege --I think--"

"In a Library" by
Emily Dickinson

You are privileged in the use of this book from
our Special Collection. You may have it for
the time checked below:

☐   In the presence of the librarian

☐   2 hours in the library

☐   Overnight loan--Due at 9:00 A.M.

☐   3-day loan

☐   7-day loan

TWO TIGERS
TAKING THE 10.20 TRAIN
TO TIMBUKTU

UNRULY UNICORNS UPENDING URNS OF ULTRAMARINE UMBRELLAS

VICTOR V. VULTURE

THE VAUDEVILLE VENTRILOQUIST

VERSATILE VIRTUOSO OF VOCIFEROUS VERBOSITY

VEXATIOUSLY VOCALIZING AT THE VALHALLA VARIETY VENUE

Wicked
Warrior
WASPS
wildly
waving
Warlike
Weapons

YOUTHFUL YAKS YODELLING
IN YELLOW YACHTS

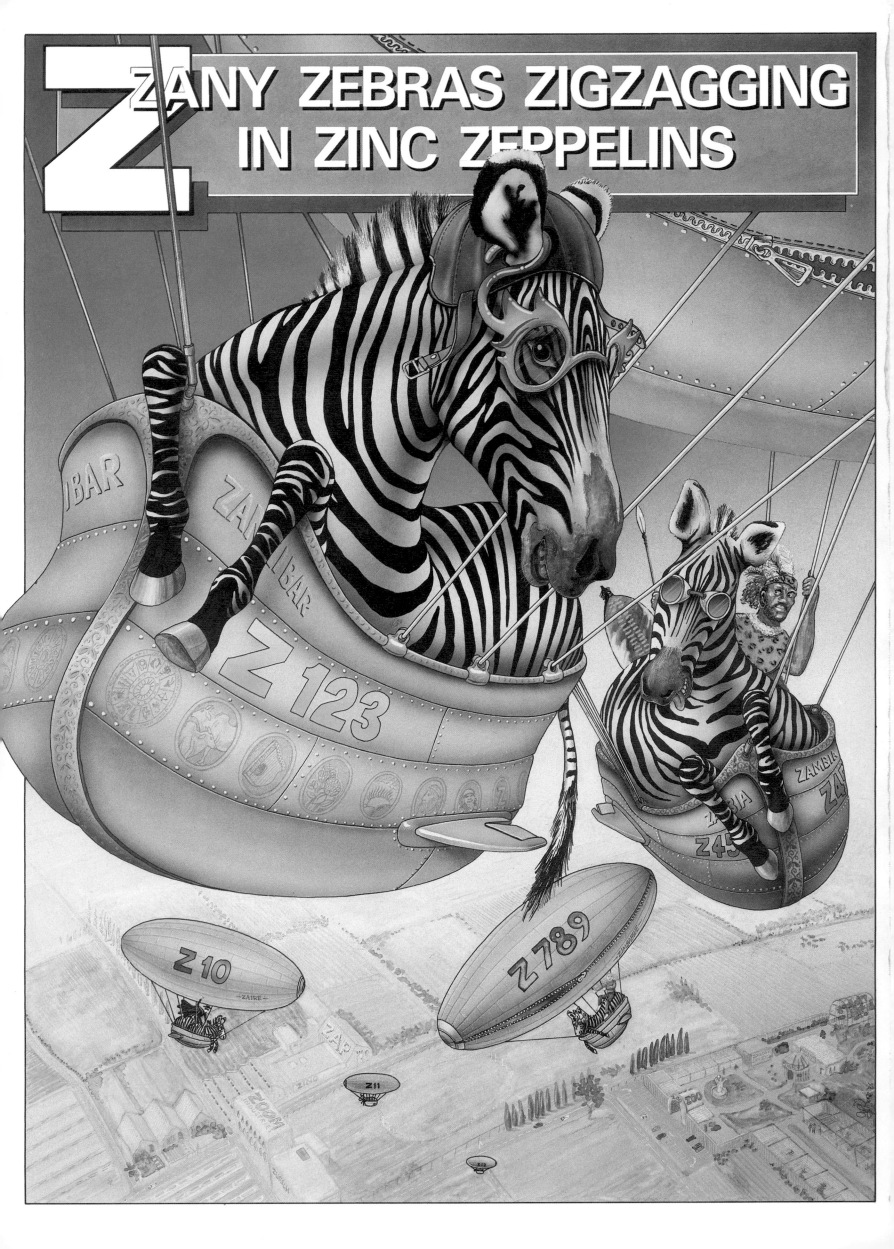

Z.
ZANY ZEBRAS ZIGZAGGING IN ZINC ZEPPELINS